The

Instant Expert's
Guide to
Single Malt Scotch

The Novice's Guide to Enjoying Single
Malt Scotch Whisky

Updated & Expanded
Second Edition

Kevin Erskine

DOCEON PRESS
RICHMOND, VIRGINIA

The Instant Expert's Guide to Single Malt Scotch
Second Edition

ISBN 0-9771991-1-8

First Printing, June 2006

PRINTED IN THE UNITED STATES OF AMERICA

DOCEON PRESS
Richmond, Virginia
www.doceonpress.com

Praise for
The Instant Expert's
Guide to Single Malt Scotch

"There are two distinct and defined trends going on in the world of whisky right now, and Kevin Erskine understands both of them. The first is a move away from pretentiousness and snobbery for all things whisky, and the other is a recommitment to the notion of drinking whisky as good fun. This book is a gem: a power punch of facts and information but presented in a total twaddle-free manner. Just like a good malt in fact, it hits the spot perfectly."

Dominic Roskrow
Editor, Whisky Magazine

"It's a great book. Straightforward, concise, matter-of-fact, no BS. Excellent. A book much needed for Scotch whisky."

John Glaser
Compass Box Whisky

"The Instant Expert's Guide to Single Malt Scotch is well-written, painstakingly researched, and comes from a true love of Scotch."

Liquorsnob.com

"Believe me, it's the best single introduction to our favorite subject that I've ever seen."

Tony Dirksen
Radio Whisky.com

Praise for
The Scotch Blog

I really like the fresh perspectives and variety of topics. A very informative and outspoken blog, updated very frequently.

Johannes van den Heuval
Malt Madness

Scotch Blog really gets it. I'm a big supporter of your efforts.

John Glaser
Compass Box Whisky

Interesting. Kind of Bible thumping, but more polite...

Jim Murray

I believe you are starting something very interesting with The Scotch Blog.

Ronnie Cox
The Glenrothes

The Scotch Blog is alarmingly well-written, offering on-target criticism from a connoisseur who is clearly passionate about his Scotch.

Bloglebrity

*This book is dedicated to my daughters
Amanda & Emily, and to Julie, who doesn't
really show her dismay that my ever-growing
single malt collection is taking over the house.*

*Thanks to Bruichladdich, Chivas Brothers, Diageo, Glencairn
Crystal, Glenmorangie, William Grant & Sons and Laphroaig
for generously providing photographs for use in this book.*

Special thanks to:

*Michael Jackson, Jim Murray, Gary Regan and David
Wishart for allowing me to reprint excerpts from their work.*

*Jakob Bruhns, John Glaser, Martine Nouet and Julie
Phillips for their assistance with the second edition.*

*Julien Gualdoni, Ethan Kelley, Mike Miller, Darcy O'Neil,
Mickael Perron, Rob Poulter and Gary Regan for allowing
me to use their signature whisky cocktail recipes.*

Malt does more than
Milton can,
To justify God's ways
to man.

A. E. Houseman, English poet

Contents

Here's to you,
as good as you are,
And here's to me,
as bad as I am;
But as good as you are,
and as bad as I am,
I am as good as you are,
as bad as I am.

Old Scottish Toast

Foreword

As you might imagine, Whisky Magazine receives many books on the subject of whisky. Some are weighty tomes, thoroughly researched and designed to be the definitive authority on their subject matter. Others have clearly been thrown together by a book company eager to exploit the current fashion for whisky in all its forms.

But there are relatively few that present the essential information required to understand and appreciate whisky in an easily accessible format and without over-intellectualising what is, at the end of the day, a drink to have fun with.

This is such a book. All the information you could possibly want to get to grips with this most fascinating of liquids but written by an enthusiast who has put a firm ban on flim-flam.

There are two distinct and defined trends going on in the world of whisky right now, and Kevin Erskine understands both of them. The first is a move away from pretentiousness and snobbery for all things whisky, and the other is a recommitment to the notion of drinking whisky as good fun. This book is a gem: a power punch of facts and information but presented in a total twaddle-free manner. Just like a good malt in fact, it hits the spot perfectly.

I'm very much a believer in the idea that someone's first experience of a subject will define their attitude to it for a long time. This book all but guarantees a soft ride in to the world of whisky – and backs it up with a great deal of relevant and pertinent information.

Dominic Roskrow
Editor, Whisky Magazine
London, England

Introduction

This book is a result of two things - my love of good single malt Scotch whisky and my experience hosting tastings for people who are interested in learning about the same.

Although my last name is Scottish, I wasn't born with a knowledge of all things Celtic. I had to make a special effort to seek out information to appreciate the rich heritage and amazing contributions to world history of my forefathers. It's not the type of thing taught in American schools.

Despite my resulting appreciation for the history and culture of Scotland, I, like many people, still had several preconceptions about Scotch whisky, including, but not limited to its flavor (terrible), and the type of people who drank it (old, stodgy, rich men).

This all changed in the early 1990s when I became involved with a local Scottish Society. One of the exhibitors at our first Highland Games was a whisky appreciation club. The seeds were planted.

It took me some time to fully appreciate the breadth and depth of single malt Scotch whisky, though I must say, I've never acquired a taste for haggis.

Years later, the rest of the world has finally started to catch up with the lovers of single malt Scotch whisky.

I guess it was inevitable that after the interest in luxury vodkas, gins and tequilas, the world would eventually turn to Scotch whisky. Why? Single malt Scotch whisky is the original luxury spirit. Scotch whisky didn't have to be created by marketing people - a wide variety of single malt Scotch whisky is aging in casks, waiting to be appreciated. As a matter of fact, most of the single malt Scotch whisky you'll be trying tomorrow was made ten or more years ago.

There's never been such a variety of easily available single malt Scotch whisky as there is right now - and, as more people acquire a taste for the stuff, the market will continue to meet the demands.

You will notice that I use *generally, usually, often* and *sometimes* an awful lot in this book. That's because there are no hard and fast rules for making (or drinking) Scotch whisky. For the most part I will describe the traditional method and note exceptions.

Also please note that in the UK, Scotch is simply referred to as "whisky" and I do the same in many parts of this book.

Will you be an expert after reading this book? Not at all. But you will have a solid foundation to start exploring single malts on your own.

It truly is a great time for you to get into Scotch whisky!

-Kevin Erskine
May, 2006

In this second edition, I've corrected some minor mistakes that made it into the first edition. I've also expanded some of the chapters and elaborated upon the basic information.

Chapter 1

The Basics

When and where the first Scottish whisky was distilled is still (in some very boring circles) a hotly debated topic. One theory contends that Irish catholic monks came to Scotland around 700 AD to spread the gospel - and brought with them the secret of turning beer into whisky.

One thing is for sure, the term 'whisky' comes from the Gaelic language, which is the ancient tongue of Scotland and Ireland. In Scots Gaelic, *Uisge Beatha*, pronounced "Ooshki Baah," translates literally as "water of life."

Regardless of where it was first made, today whisky is produced all over the globe. You can find whisk(e)y distilleries in Scotland, Ireland, Wales, France, Germany, Switzerland, Canada, the U.S., Australia, New Zealand, India, Thailand, South Africa, and Japan.

But *single malt* **Scotch** *whisky* is made in only one place. Or rather, it is made in many places, but only in one country - Scotland.

Whisky vs. Whiskey

There's a bit of confusion over the correct spelling of whisky, so let's get this out of the way right up front. You will come across two distinct spellings for the word - one with an 'e' (*whiskey*) and one without (*whisky*).

When a whisky is produced in Scotland it is ALWAYS spelled *whisky*. You will search long and hard and find no reason why this is so. Though knowing how the Scottish hold a grudge, I wouldn't be surprised if it had something to do with pulling the 'e' to insult England!

Japan and Canada also generally use the *whisky* spelling, while in Ireland and the U.S. it is usually, but not always, spelled with an 'e', as *whiskey*.

When someone is trying to be inclusive and refer to all types of whiskies, they'll often use the spelling *whisk(e)y*.

American whiskey

You may not know it, but there is a legal definition for the term "whisky" in the United States. This definition is taken from the *U.S. Code of Federal Regulations, Title 27, Part 5: Subpart C: Standards of Identity for Distilled Spirits*:

> *"Whisky" is an alcoholic distillate from a fermented mash of grain produced at less than 190° proof in such manner that the distillate possesses the taste, aroma, and characteristics generally attributed to whisky, stored in oak containers (except that corn whisky need not be so stored), and bottled at not less than 80° proof.*

You may have noticed in the above passage that *whisky* is spelled without an 'e'. That is not a misprint. The U.S. Congress enshrined the *whisky* spelling into law.

Bourbon

When most people think American whiskey, they think **Bourbon.** By law, *straight Bourbon whiskey* is a whiskey which is distilled at no higher than 160° proof (80% alcohol by volume or *ABV*) from a fermented mash (more on this later) of not less than 51% corn*, and stored at not more than 125° proof (62.5% ABV) in charred, new oak containers for a period of 2 years or more. It may not be bottled at less than 80° proof (40% ABV).

It is absolutely **not** true that only whiskey distilled in Kentucky can be called bourbon. Bourbon refers to a type of whiskey, not where the whiskey is made. The name comes from the county in Kentucky where this particular style of whiskey was first made.

Tennessee Whiskey is made in much the same way as bourbon. The difference is in the *Lincoln County Process* whereby after distillation, the whiskey is slowly filtered through sugar maple charcoal. This adds a sweet and sooty character to the whiskey as it removes impurities.

American whiskies that are made primarily from rye or wheat are also seeing a resurgence. In the U.S. rye whiskey, wheat whiskey, or rye malt whiskey are whiskies that are produced from a fermented mash of not less than 51% rye, wheat, or malted rye grain, respectively; do not exceed 160° proof, and are stored at not more than 125° proof in charred, new oak containers for a period of 2 years or more.

Irish whiskey

There are several excellent brands of single malt Irish whiskey, but the better known brands are the blends (such as Jameson, Tullamore Dew and Bushmills).

---

*The remaining 49% of the "mash bill" can be barley, rye and/or wheat. All Bourbons include some percentage of malted barley which helps activate the enzymes in the other grains.

Aside from the extra 'e', there are some very specific differences between the processes for making Irish and Scotch whiskies.

- Irish distillers traditionally do not use peat smoke to dry their barley. Instead, barley for Irish whiskey is dried using hot air in closed ovens. Smoke never comes into contact with the malted barley.
- Irish whiskey can vary in its composition, but generally uses a mixture of malted and unmalted barley which is distilled in pot-stills. The grain portion of Irish blends is predominately corn (though both unmalted barley and wheat have been used) and distilled in a "continuous still".
- Irish whiskey is usually distilled three times, while Scotch whisky is distilled twice.

These differences result in a lighter and arguably smoother (some say "more bland") flavor.

Why Irish whiskey distillers do not take advantage of the massive amounts of peat on their island is a mystery, though *Cooley*, one of the three Irish Distillers, is producing peated whiskies.

Legally Speaking

Originally, the definitions for Scotch whisky were quite loose. The first attempt to codify terms was by the British *Royal Commission on Whiskey* who, in 1909, decided that the term whiskey "could be applied to a product of malt and grain, including maize (corn)" This meant that any sort of grain was fair game when making whiskey.

Notice the spelling - the Royal Commission used the *whiskey* spelling in all of it's findings. It's only fairly recently - the early 20th century - that the *whisky* spelling has become the convention in Scotland. It's also interesting that there is no law in any country which dictates which spelling must be used.

A few years after the Royal Commission concluded their findings, the *Immature Spirits Act of 1915* was passed and declared that whisky must be aged in a "wooden cask" for a minimum of two years - in 1916 this was extended to a minimum of three years.

It wasn't until 1990 that the *Scotch Whisky Order,* an amendment to the 1988 *Scotch Whisky Act,* specified that **oak** was the only type of wood to be used during maturation.

With the Scotch Whisky Order, the legal definition of single malt Scotch whisky has been codified:

- An alcoholic beverage made from water and malted barley. It may be fermented only through the addition of yeast.
- The mash must be processed in Scotland, the spirit must be distilled in Scotland and the whisky must be matured in a warehouse in Scotland.
- The distillation can not exceed 94.8 % alcohol by volume, and the distillate must have "an aroma and taste derived from the raw materials used in, and the method of, its production."
- The distillate must be matured "in oak casks of a capacity not exceeding 700 litres - the period of that maturation being not less than 3 years."

- The maturation must ensure that the whisky "retains the colour, aroma and taste derived from the raw materials used in, and the method of, its production and maturation, and to which no substance other than water and spirit caramel has been added."
- The 1990 Scotch Whisky Order also added the specification that Scotch whisky must be bottled at a minimum strength of 40% ABV.
- Most interestingly, the Scotch Whisky Act 1988 prohibits the production of any type of whisky in Scotland other than Scotch Whisky. That is, you cannot make bourbon-style whiskey in Scotland.

Types of Whisky

Single Malt: A single malt is a whisky made only from malted barley (and no other grains) and distilled in a single distillery.

Pure Malt/Vatted Malt: Confusing terms for a whisky produced by mixing single malts from different distilleries. - Under new guidelines from the Scotch Whisky Association, these are now to be referred to as **Blended Malts**.

Blended Whisky: A mix of malt whisky (generally from different distilleries) and non-malted grain whisky.

Grain Whisky: A whisky made from grains - usually wheat, corn or unmalted barley, and produced in a patent still (also called a continuous or Coffey still).

How to read a single malt Scotch label

Distillery

People sometimes mistakenly refer to the distillery name as the *brand*. Single malts are generally named after the distillery in which they are made, while blends, including blended malts, use brand names.

Region & Type

Sometimes the region and type are listed together, sometimes separately. Bruichladdich is a **single malt** from the **Islay** region.

BRUICHLADDICH

ISLAY SINGLE MALT
SCOTCH WHISKY

Fifteen
AGED YEARS

70cl e   DISTILLED & MATURED AT BRUICHLADDICH DISTILLERY
                             ISLAY SCOTLAND   46%vol

Age Statement

Should be prominently displayed.

Alcohol content

Shown as a percentage and not as a *proof.*

If you remember nothing else...

The term *single malt Scotch whisky* refers to a whisky which is:

1. Distilled in Scotland at a single distillery, and
2. Made from malted barley, with no other grains.

This distinguishes *single malt* **Scotch whisky** from all other whiskies which are:

1. Distilled outside of Scotland (regardless of the ingredients) and
2. Those whiskies distilled in Scotland, but which are created by either blending single malts from multiple distillers (called "Blended" or "Vatted" Malt) or by blending single malt Scotch whisky with grain whisky (called "Blended Scotch" or "Blended Scotch Whisky").

Chapter 2

How It's Made

How single malt is made (In a nutshell)

Single malt is produced from malted barley. The barley is soaked in water and allowed to germinate. It is then dried using smoke from a fire which (usually) has had peat added. The malted barley is then ground into grist, mixed with water, and allowed to ferment through the addition of yeast. The resulting liquid is distilled (twice) in copper *pot stills*, and matured in oak casks for at least three years. Once bottled, whisky, unlike wine, does not continue to age or change, provided the bottle is kept sealed and out of sunlight.

How single malt is made (More than you needed to know)

Barley, yeast, and water are the sole ingredients required for making single malt Scotch whisky. Some people contend that peat is an ingredient. Since you can certainly make whisky without peat, I submit that it is not so much an ingredient as an additive.

It all starts with barley, a plentiful crop in Scotland. There are a number of varieties of barley that may be used when making whisky, but the consensus among distillers is that

---

the variety of barley used makes no difference in the flavor of the resulting whisky.

I'll be describing the traditional method for distilling single malt Scotch whisky, though in actual practice there is much variation, and automation has been introduced by many of the larger distillers. The basic process consists of: Malting, Mashing, Fermentation, Distillation, Aging/Maturation, and Bottling.

Malting

The barley is soaked in water for several days, then transferred to a malting floor where it is spread out to germinate for about a week.

SCIENCE ALERT! The malting process is all about getting the barley to the point of germination - this allows enzymes in the barley to turn starch into soluble sugars, which will convert to alcohol later in the process.

The barley is periodically *turned* by running a rake called a *shiel* through the germinating barley.

Only a few distillers (Balvenie, Bowmore, Highland Park, Laphroaig, and Springbank among them) still malt their own barley - the majority now use malted barley supplied by commercial maltsters, who will peat the barley to the distillery's specifications. Even among those distilleries that continue to malt their own barley, some have moved to an automated malting process.

When the barley begins to sprout, it is moved to a smoking room where smoke from a kiln below is used to heat the air, drying the barley and quickly stopping the germination process.

Peat (a mixture of partially decomposed moss and other organic matter that forms in wetlands, which when dried can be used as fuel) *may be*, and for most single malts *is*, added to the kiln to give the barley the characteristic peaty (earthy/smoky) flavor. But not all distillers use peat, and when used, it is in varying degrees. (Islay whiskies are traditionally more heavily peated, while Lowland whiskies may use very little or none.)

After being heated in the kiln, the barley is then allowed to continue to air dry.

Mashing

Once dried, the malted barley is crushed in a mill and turned into a coarse flour called *grist* to prepare it for the next phase - mashing.

The barley grist is then mixed with water (from a natural source such as a river, spring, or stream) which has been heated to 150° Fahrenheit in a large vessel called a *mash tun*.

The Scottish water plays a role in the subsequent flavor of the whisky - but just as importantly, the hot water activates the conversion of starch into sugar.

The resulting sugary water (known as *wort*) is then cooled to room temperature and transferred to a *wash back*, a large vessel made of either wood or stainless steel. The more traditional distillers prefer wood, as they believe the bacteria in the wood enhances the flavor.

Fermentation

Yeast is added to the wash back to begin fermentation. Alcohol is the result of the fermentation process - a microorganism (yeast) feeds on the sugars and converts them into alcohol and carbon dioxide gas.

The process of fermentation takes anywhere from two to four days and results in a liquid known as *wash* which has an alcohol content of between 8-10%.

At this point about two weeks have passed since the malting process began and so far it hasn't been much different than the production of beer.

Distillation

This is where the real magic begins.

Distillation is the process of separating the compounds in a liquid by heating the liquid to its vapor point and then condensing the vapor into a purified and/or concentrated liquid form.

In the case of fermented liquids, distillation creates a more powerful version; distilling beer gives us whisky just as distilling wine gives us brandy.

Single malts are distilled in a *pot still* which is basically a very large pear/onion-shaped kettle made of copper. Pot stills allow for distillation to occur in batches, as opposed to a continuous still, which is used for the distillation of most other liquors.

Single malts actually go through two distillations. While originally a single still was used for both distillations, today two separate pot stills are used.

The first distillation takes place in a still called a *wash still*.

Pot Stills at Laphroaig

The wash is heated to a temperature of 170° Fahrenheit (the boiling point of alcohol) which causes the alcohol in the wash to vaporize. The vapor travels up through the neck of the still, through the *lyne arm*, into a condenser which has been immersed in cool water. While traveling through the condenser, the vapor cools and condenses back into a liquid with an alcohol content of about 25%. This liquid is called a *low wine.*

The low wine is put through a second distillation (which takes place in a separate pot still called a *spirit still)* to refine it further. Distilling a second time not only removes more impurities, but also raises the alcohol content to about 70%. This liquid, called *new make spirit* can finally be called **whisky** after proper aging.

The size and shape of the pot still, including the shape and length of the neck, even the angle of the lyne arm, are major factors in the character of the resulting whisky. Lighter and fruitier flavors come from a narrower still with

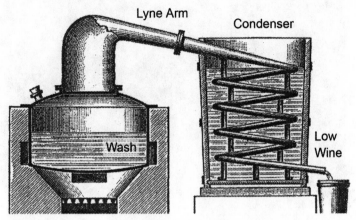

Lyne Arm

Condenser

Wash

Low
Wine

The distilling process - turning wash into low wine

a longer neck, while a short, stout still with a shorter neck tends to generate richer flavors.

SCIENCE ALERT! This makes perfect sense once you understand that heavier flavor compounds have a higher boiling point than lighter compounds. As the vapors created from heavier compounds rise up a tall neck, they can cool and condense back into a liquid before reaching the condenser, dropping back into the still. As a result, heavier flavor compounds sometimes do not make it into the final product. A short neck allows the richer flavors to continue through the condenser before reverting to liquid.

Aging/Maturation

Only oak is used to mature single malt Scotch whisky. The use of oak was not a legal dictate until 1990, but oak has been used for many, many years. It was discovered that oak barrels were sturdy enough to hold whisky through the

How It's Made

extended maturation process, and more importantly, the oak adds substantially to the flavor of single malt Scotch whisky. It has been asserted that whisky gains 60-70% of its character from the oak casks in which it has been matured. This means that the wooden cask has a greater effect on the flavor of the end product than barley, water, peat and still shape combined.

About 90% of single malt Scotch whisky distilled in Scotland is aged in casks made of American white oak which were previously used to age bourbon. The wide spread use of bourbon barrels is a fairly recent occurrence - a result of the difficulty in sourcing sherry casks during the Spanish civil war in the late 1930's. Currently anywhere from 300,000 - 400,000 bourbon casks are acquired annually for use in the maturation of Scotch whisky - in contrast to only about 18,000 sherry casks.

Before they are used to mature bourbon, the casks are thoroughly *charred* - the inside of the cask is set on fire for a short period of time, which creates a black, charred layer. There are various levels of charring which will have different affects on the spectrum of compounds and flavors the oak will impart to the maturing spirit, but the main result of the char is to produce a sweet vanilla-like aroma.

Since bourbon casks may, by US law, only be used once, and since brand new, unused oak casks would overpower the subtleties of new make spirit, an opportunity is created for both distillers of bourbon (who get to recoup some of the investment in casks) and distillers of single malt Scotch whisky (who get to take advantage of a stable supply of previously used bourbon casks).

Whisky Production

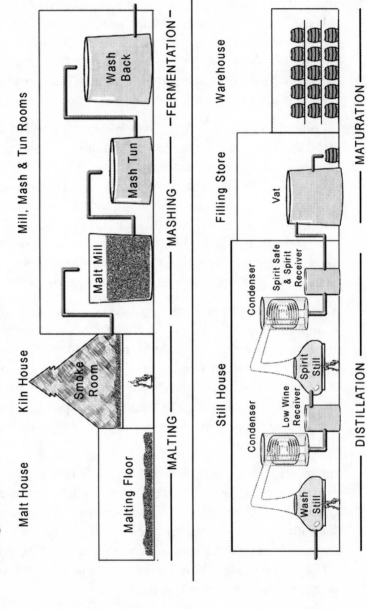

Malt House   Kiln House   Mill, Mash & Tun Rooms

Smoke Room

Malting Floor

— MALTING —   — MASHING —   — FERMENTATION —

Malt Mill   Mash Tun   Wash Back

Still House   Filling Store   Warehouse

Condenser   Condenser   Spirit Safe & Spirit Receiver   Vat

Wash Still   Low Wine Receiver   Spirit Still

— DISTILLATION —   — MATURATION —

The aging bourbon softens the wood, so that the woody flavors in the cask will not overpower the single malt, yet the bourbon does not impart new flavors to the single malt.

The previously used bourbon casks also give the Scotch whisky a golden color, which can vary in intensity according to the age of the cask and the length of maturation.

Some distillers, notably Macallan, primarily use casks made of Spanish oak which had previously contained maturing sherry. These casks are not charred and retain much of the sherry flavor. This results in a significantly different tasting whisky with sweeter, spicier overtones and a rich, dark amber color. However, sherry casks are far less common than bourbon casks and quite a bit more expensive.

Contrary to popular belief, very few whiskies are aged exclusively in bourbon barrels - most single malts are vatted with a (varying) percentage of whisky which was aged in ex-sherry barrels. Laphroaig, Glemorangie 10, Ardbeg 10, and Glenlivet 12 are among those few "pure" whiskies - those aged only in bourbon barrels.

Aging Sherry casks

Bourbon casks are relatively small, with a capacity of 180 liters (47.5 gallons), while the larger sherry casks holds 500 liters (132 gallons). Casks of both types are generally discarded after being used for only one or two fills, but may be used three or even four times. Even two fills can equate to a working lifetime of 22 years or more.

Scotch whisky MUST be matured in a cask for at least 3 years before it can legally be called whisky - though most single malts which will be bottled and sold are matured for at least ten years and often longer.

One unfortunate side effect of housing the maturing whisky in wooden casks is the rate of evaporation. Two percent or more of the volume in a cask may be lost *each year*. This loss is quaintly referred to as "the Angel's Share."

Any whisky aged ten years or longer will very likely display the age of the whisky prominently on the bottle. You can be sure that any single malt that does NOT have an age clearly visible on the bottle has been aged at least three years, but less than ten years.

There are a number of vatted (or blended) malts being introduced which do not declare their age. This is because at least one (and likely more) of the single malts in the blend is less than ten years old. Some of these vatted malts are aimed directly at the novice, and the lack of an age statement in a blend should not worry you too much.

Finishing
A recent trend in single malts is *finishing*. After the initial aging the whisky is removed from its original cask and matured in a second cask that had previously contained a spirit such as sherry, wine, cognac or even rum.

Bottles which have been finished should be clearly labeled with the previous contents and/or type of wood of the finishing cask. The finishing will take place over an additional six months to two years, but the time spent in the finishing process is generally not displayed on the bottle label.

Finished whiskies undeniably take on additional flavors and an added dimension. Far from being a fad, I believe more distillers will introduce finished products.

Bottling

Vatting

Vatting is a term used to describe a technique where the contents of different casks are mixed prior to bottling. This is a common practice in whisky production, and a single bottle will contain whisky from several casks - even casks distilled in different years.

Vatting is common in the production of blends, pure/blended malts, and single malts.

Glenmorangie and Balvenie are two distillers that have experimented extensively with finishing.

Yes, that's right, single malts. What few people realize is that most single malts *are*, in fact, vatted. The average bottle of single malt Scotch whisky is produced from the contents of a number of different casks - all of which are products of the same distillery.

The reason that vatting is so common is that whisky distillation is an art as well as a science. Like wine, the distillations from different years can have different characteristics. Unlike wine, however, single malt Scotch whisky distillers do not release a specific year's product (with the exception of a *Single Cask* bottling). As a result, they mix the distillations from different years in order to create a product that is as consistent as possible. Distillers may also legally add small amounts of coloring (in the form of spirit caramel) in order to ensure that each batch has a consistent color.

Two things you can be sure of when picking up a bottle of that is labeled as a **single malt Scotch whisky**:

1. The age listed on the bottle is the age of the youngest whisky in the bottle. If your bottle says "10 Year Old," you can be sure that all of the whiskies in that bottle are *at least* ten years old; and

2. It is all single malt from the same distillery.

Dilution
Most single malt bottlings are reduced to between 40-46% (80-92 proof) alcohol by volume by adding water prior to bottling. A *Cask Strength* bottling is a notable exception.

Special bottlings

Single Cask

A Scotch whisky is referred to as a "single cask" when the contents of only one cask of single malt Scotch whisky are used for that particular bottling. Generally the date of distillation, the date or month of bottling, and the number of bottles drawn from the cask are indicated on the label.

Again, unless you are drinking single malt Scotch whisky that has been drawn from a single cask, a number of different casks will have been vatted together.

Balvenie Single Barrel - a single cask

Cask Strength

A growing number of distillers are releasing *cask strength* bottlings.

The term refers to the alcohol content of the whisky when taken directly from the cask, without the addition of water. As a result, they have an alcohol content anywhere between 50% and 60% (and sometimes higher).

It is important to note that as whisky matures in a cask evaporation causes a reduction in the alcohol content - so a very old cask strength bottling could have a comparatively low percentage of alcohol.

A single cask bottling is not necessarily cask strength and may be diluted before being bottled. Likewise a cask strength bottling is not necessarily a single cask bottling But there *are* single cask, cask strength bottlings.

Proper storage

Unlike wine, malt whisky does not continue to mature once it has been removed from the cask and bottled.

Interestingly, an unopened bottle of single malt Scotch whisky should remain very much the same as when it was bottled, regardless of the time spent in the bottle - assuming that the bottle was stored correctly and kept out of direct sunlight.

Some people will tell you that once opened, a bottle of single malt must be consumed within a certain period of time.

While this is a good rule of thumb, I have some bottles which have been opened for years and I can detect no degradation in them. Several open bottles have actually improved substantially over the years.

Once opened and exposed to air, whisky *may* degrade - the extent of degradation is completely dependent on the whisky and the storage conditions.

If you need me to draw a line in the sand, try this: once a bottle is more than half empty, it should be finished within 18 months. But remember, there's simply no hard and fast rule for consumption that can be relied upon for every bottle.

Most single malt Scotch whisky bottles are sold in a cardboard box or tube called a "presentation carton." The carton is more than just pretty packaging - it is designed to protect the bottle's contents from exposure to light. If you are not storing your whisky in an enclosed bar or cupboard, it is a good idea to store any single malt you purchase in its carton.

Stored whisky should not be exposed to extremes of temperature. Storing your bottles at "cellar temperature," about 65-67 degrees Fahrenheit (18.3-19.4 degrees Celsius), is ideal.

Unlike wine, Scotch whisky should not be stored on its side - whisky should always be stored in a standing position to avoid continuous contact with the cork.

Final note

There are some 90 distilleries making whisky in Scotland, – but a number of those distillers do not bottle their product. The product of these distilleries is created to make blended Scotch whisky. By selling only to blenders, the distillery does not have to worry about bottling, labeling, distribution, or marketing.

There are independent bottlers who will buy casks of mature whisky from these distilleries and release a limited bottling under their own label.

A bottling that is packaged and sold by a distiller under their own label is referred to as an OB or *Original Bottling*, while a bottling sold by an Independent Bottler is referred to as an IB or *Independent Bottling*.

If you remember nothing else...

Single malt Scotch whisky is *basically* distilled beer.

Single malt Scotch whisky is traditionally double distilled.

Scotch whisky MUST be matured in a cask for at least 3 years before it can legally be called whisky.

Very few whiskies are aged exclusively in bourbon barrels - most single malts are vatted with a percentage of whisky which was aged in ex-sherry barrels.

Casks are generally used only once or twice before being retired, but may be used as many as four times.

The age on the label is the age of the youngest whisky in the bottle.

Unless the bottle is labeled as *cask strength* it's usually been diluted to 40-46% alcohol.

Even single malts are vatted unless they state that they are Single Cask.

Whisky stops maturing once bottled.

Chapter 3
What About Wood?

The interaction between wood and maturing whisky is one of the most interesting, if not completely understood, components of the whisky production process. The science surrounding the topic is quite complex, and though I've attempted to boil down the important points regarding the impact that wood has on the maturing whisky, it really is a topic that defies easy summary.

As stated earlier, Scotch whisky gains anywhere from 60-70% of its flavor, and all of its color*, from oak casks. But a question many people have is "Why do whisky makers use oak?"

Oak is utilized because of its unique physical and chemical nature: 1. oak has strength - physically, its wide radial rays give strength when shaped for a cask, and 2. oak is a "pure wood", as opposed to pine or rubber trees which contain resin canals that can pass strong flavors to maturing whisky.

But it's not just the oak itself, it's the transformation that happens to oak as a result of the seasoning and heating treatments during the coopering process - these result in pleasant-tasting flavors.

---

* *Except for those whiskies that have been artificially colored through the addition of spirit caramel.*

Will any oak do?

No. Of the hundreds of species of oak, just three species are used for wine and whisky cooperage:

Quercus Alba, "White oak" (America)
White oak is commonly referred to as *American oak* and is the most commonly used variety in whisky cooperage.

Quercus Petraea, "Sessile oak" (Europe)
Sessile oak is found across Europe, most notably in France, and is commonly used in the construction of barrels destined to store wine. The most common variety used is the species found in the Tronçais forest.

Quercus Robur, "Pedunculate oak" (Europe)
Pedunculate oak is also found throughout Europe (but is commonly called *Spanish oak*) and is commonly used for cognac and sherry maturation. The most common variety is found in the Limousin forest.

Other factors

There are several additional factors affecting how wood impacts whisky. Chief among these factors are the growth rate of the "donor trees", the method and length of time to dry the wood, and the toasting and charring methods during cooperage.

Slower is better (Growth rate)

Wine makers are convinced of the relationship between oak growth rates and the flavor and quality of their wines.

It is well known within the wine industry that slow growth oak has more of the "good stuff" - especially vanillins and oak lactones. In the whisky industry, however, the impact of growth rates is not widely considered.

White oak is a fast growth variety which has more vanillin than its European cousins and is high in lactones which, when toasted, provide woody, vanilla, and coconut flavors. Sessile oak is a slow growth species, resulting in fine tannins and more vanilla. Pedunculate oak is a fast growth species resulting in more tannins when compared to Sessile oak.

Tis' the season (Seasoning)

Once the wood is cut, the method used to season (or dry) the wood has a huge impact. The wood **must** be dried before being used to make barrels - the drying process converts chemical compounds in the wood to more desirable types. But how the wood is dried and for how long has a direct impact on the quality of the spirit.

It is widely accepted that air seasoning is better than kiln drying, yet, while the barrels used to age wine may be made of staves which have been air dried for as much as 24 months, most bourbon barrels are made from wood which has been kiln dried over a matter of weeks.

The reason for this is that some distillers think that the method for drying the wood is only important for the first-fill of a spirit aged in a new cask, (e.g., wine or bourbon) and has little or no impact when maturing spirits in previously used casks - and of course, Scotch whisky is aged in previously used casks.

The heat is on (Toasting/Charring)

The application of heat is integral to the process of making a barrel. Wood fibers want to be straight, so in order to bend the staves, they need to be heated.

To do this, the straight staves are arranged inside a metal hoop and heated, either an open flame or steam may be used. As the staves are heated they become more pliable and are bent into shape - hoops of various diameters are added to each end and hammered down towards the middle to keep the staves in place. Each hoop is held in place by the pressure exerted by the staves as they try to straighten themselves. The casks are then toasted, which caramelizes the wood sugars.

This is where the construction of bourbon casks and sherry casks diverge.

Bourbon casks

Bourbon casks, once formed, are *charred* - this is the act of setting the inside of the cask on fire for a short period of time, creating a black charred layer. The result of charring is a dramatic change to the exposed surface - wood sugars are caramelized which will leech into the maturing spirit.

Bourbon casks are typically charred from 40 seconds to 1 minute, but some distilleries have experimented with charring times of up to 3 or 4 minutes. Different charring levels will have different impacts on the flavors the cask will impart to the maturing spirit.

Once charred, the cask is ready to be filled with bourbon and will be allowed to mature for two or more years. Once a bourbon cask has completed this "first life" - it is ready for its second life as a whisky aging container.

The cask is broken back down into separate staves and shipped to Scotland, where coopers will reassemble the casks. Though it is not common, some distillers may re-char bourbon casks before use. The cask is now ready to mature Scotch for (at least) the next three years.

Sherry casks

Sherry Casks take a slightly different path - most notably, they are not charred. Without a char, there is less carmelization of the sugars and as a result, less vanilla flavor is passed to the maturing spirit.

The casks are then ready to mature sherry, which must be aged for at least 3 years, though the finer sherries are aged for much longer. After they've completed this job, the casks are shipped to Scotland whole - unlike bourbon casks, they are not broken down into separate staves.

Whisky distillers will empty the sherry cask of any residual sherry, nose the cask (to ensure the casks smells fresh) and then fill with new make spirit.

The species of oak used in the construction of sherry casks (Quercus Robur) has a bigger influence on the whisky than the sherry the cask contained. Spanish Oak has a finer grain than white oak, producing more tannins and less lactones than its American cousin. This means that while bourbon casks tend to soften the raw spirit and add vanilla and caramel flavors, sherry casks tends to bring more fullness to the flavor, with spicy and nutty notes.

If you remember nothing else...

Scotch whisky gains anywhere from 60-70% of its flavor, and all of its color (aside from those whiskies which have had artificial color added) from oak casks.

By law, only oak is used to mature Scotch whisky, though this law has only been in place since 1990.

About 90% of Scotch whisky is aged in casks made of white American oak which had previously been used to age bourbon.

The remainder is aged in casks made of Spanish oak which had previously been used to age sherry.

White oak adds vanilla and caramel flavors, while Spanish oak tends to bring more fullness to the flavor, with prune, raisin, spice and nutty notes.

What About Wood?

Chapter 4

Where It's Made

There seems to be some confusion about the number of whisky-producing regions in Scotland and their geographic boundaries. Various sources cite four, five or even six separate regions.

For our purposes, we'll talk about four major whisky-producing regions in Scotland:

Speyside	**Islay**
Highland	**Lowland**

The Regions

Speyside

Historically considered to be a part of the Highland region, almost half of Scotland's malt whisky distilleries cluster along the river Spey and its tributaries.

With so many distilleries in a fairly small area, the region is sometimes further divided into sub regions such as Elgin, the Upper Spey, Dufftown and Glenrothes. We'll limit ourselves to just *Speyside*, and separate the region from other Highland distilleries.

With many of the best known single malts produced in this area, Speyside is acknowledged as the heart of malt distillation.

The whisky producing regions of Scotland

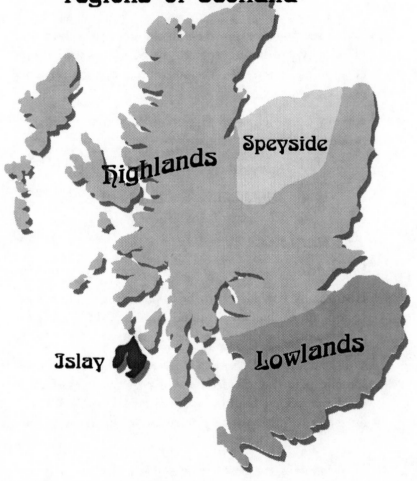

Highlands

Speyside

Islay

Lowlands

With so many distilleries, it is hard to point to distinct similarities among them. Speyside malts offer quite a spectrum of flavors. Even among the cluster of sherry cask aged whiskies of note (Macallan, Glenfarclas, and Aberlour) there are distinct variations.

Some of the better known Speyside distilleries:

Aberlour	Glenfiddich
Balvenie	The Glenlivet
Cragganmore	Macallan

Highlands

The Highlands of Scotland are known for their ruggedness and harsh climate. Yet still, there are few commonalities we can point to among the whiskies from this region.

As a matter of fact, geographically, the area is quite large and there are more differences than similarities among the products of these distilleries.

Even when breaking down the Highlands further into North, West, East, and Central sub-regions it's difficult to classify by common characteristics.

The Highlands classification includes the whiskies produced on the surrounding islands - with the notable exception of Islay, which is a production region on its own.

Some Highland distilleries:

Dalmore	Glenmorangie
Dalwhinnie	Oban
Edradour	Talisker

Islay

The island of Islay (pronounced 'Eye-luh') is the southernmost of the Western Isles. It is very largely covered in peat - the water on the island is brown with it. The island is hammered by sea-borne winter gales, blowing sea salt far inland, saturating the peat, which is subsequently dried by the salty, sea weedy breeze - you can taste the sea in an Islay whisky.

Peat is used liberally in most, but not all, Islay whiskies, and this region, unlike the others, is associated with a truly distinctive style. Islay whiskies have a smell and taste that has variously been described as iodine, brine, seaweed, and medicinal. The more peated Islay malts are generally acknowledged to be an acquired taste - most people either love 'em or hate 'em.

Yet, despite the common perception, not all whisky on Islay can be classified as smoky and peaty - Bruichladdich's 10 year old and Bunnahabhain's 12 year old are remarkably delicate, and could easily be confused with your average Speyside.

Though the island is only 25 miles long, it has eight working distilleries. A ninth distillery, Port Ellen, is no longer actively distilling. The newest distillery, *Kilchoman*, the first to be built on Islay in 124 years, only recently began production.

The Islay distilleries:

Ardbeg	Bunnahabhain	Lagavulin
Bowmore	Caol Ila	Laphroaig
Bruichladdich	Kilchoman	

Lowlands

There was a time in the 1850s, when every town of any size in the Lowlands had a distillery to supply the English market and local demands. Now, few remain.

This area tends to produce whiskies which taste more of malt, with little or no peating, and very little evidence of salt air or seaweed. The Lowland whiskies tend to be softer and mellower than their highland counterparts. The Lowland distilleries at one time all used the triple distillation method, which was a big factor in the lighter, smoother flavor - today only Auchentoshan continues to triple distill.

The Lowland distilleries:

Auchentoshan   Bladnoch   Glenkinchie

What about Campbeltown?

You'll likely hear about a region called Campbeltown. At one time it was very much a region unto itself. From the 1880s through the 1920s there were 34 working distilleries in and around the town. Today, only two distilleries are producing, **Springbank** and **Glen Scotia**. Nothing wrong with these distilleries, but in my book, two distilleries without a distinct and common style, does not a region make. Springbank and Glen Scotia disagree with me, and proudly claim Campbeltown as their region of origin.

And the Islands?

Fairly recently, there has been a movement to define a new region called the *Islands*. The term refers to all of the whisky-producing islands (except Islay) of Scotland - Skye, Jura, Orkney, Arran, & Mull. These islands are geographically dispersed around the perimeter of Scotland, and because of this, as well as the lack of an identifiable style among the distilleries, I will not treat them a separate region, but include them instead with the Highlands.

I asked Jim Murray (well-known whisky expert and author of Jim Murray's Whiskey Bible) his views on the Islands:

> *"Islands. No, I have never regarded them as a region mainly because their styles do vary. No other island, for instance, produces the honey thread one finds in both Highland Park and Scapa. Some island whiskies produce recently peated drams, like on Jura and Mull; and historically like on Skye. And where does Arran fit in with those? Doesn't really."*

A new distillery, *Blackwood*, was announced several years ago with plans to be built in the Shetland islands. As of this writing, construction has not yet begun.

My take

Choosing whiskies based on region is simply not the best way to start your journey into the world of whisky.

My experience has shown that there are more differences among the vast majority of the regionally associated distilleries than there are similarities. As a result, I rely on the regions for understanding whisky from a geographic and historical perspective and not necessarily as an indicator for what to expect when trying the whisky.

If you remember nothing else...

Four regions: Highlands, Speyside, Islay, & Lowlands.

Campbeltown and the Islands are sometimes referred to as regions; Campbeltown traditionally and the Islands recently.

Speyside has the largest concentration of distilleries, as well as some of the better known whiskies.

Highland whiskies are difficult to characterize due to great variations in styles and geography.

While Islay produces some of the more peated whiskies, despite common misconception, not all are heavily peated.

The Lowlands produce some of the lightest whiskies.

> The light music of whisky falling into a glass - an agreeable interlude.
>
> *James Joyce, Author*

Chapter 5

How To Taste It

Tasting single malt Scotch (In a nutshell)

There are three basic attributes to observe when tasting Scotch whisky (single malt or otherwise):

Appearance: the color and general look

Nose: the aromas

Taste & Finish: the flavors you detect while drinking and those you detect after drinking.

The traditional glass for a whisky tasting is a tulip-shaped glass, which allows the aroma to gather in the bell of the glass, and concentrates it (by way of the smaller mouth) for the nosing. A brandy style snifter also works well for tasting.

The only thing single malt drinkers add to their whisky is a bit of water, but even connoisseurs have differences in opinion on how much is appropriate - I've heard the entire spectrum, from a few drops all the way to a 50/50 dilution. I suggest that you start with a few drops and let your personal taste dictate how much more water to add.

When tasting single malt Scotch whisky, ice or soda water should never be added - not only will they mask the taste, they can destroy it.

Tasting single malt Scotch
(More than you need to know)

Proper tasting glasses

Let's discuss the appropriate glass to use when tasting single malt Scotch whisky. But first, a brief history lesson.

Malt whisky was, at one time, considered to be a "wild & fiery" drink, appropriate only for the Highlander. In the 1800s, enterprising businessmen decided to tame the rich flavors of malt whisky for the more delicate palates of Europe. This was accomplished by mixing the stronger single malt with milder whiskies made from grains which had been distilled in a new type of still known as a continuous still.

This whisky, known as "blended Scotch," became quite popular in the later 19th century, and was usually taken with ice and soda water - a custom which continues today.

"Rocks" glass

The glass favored by blended whisky drinkers is a short, cylindrical tumbler, usually referred to as a Scotch or "rocks" glass. This type of glass is fine for drinking a blend with some ice, but is completely unsuited for the subtlety of malt whisky.

The rocks glass does nothing to enhance the whisky drinking experience, it is simply a glass that is readily available at bars, restaurants, and in the average home.

A tulip-shaped tasting glass is the ideal vessel for tasting a single malt. Why? David Wishart, author of *Whisky Classified* says it best:

> *To truly savor all that a single malt has to offer, the proper shape is of the utmost importance.*
>
> *The nosing glass used in the whisky industry is tulip shaped like a sherry glass with a narrow mouth...The narrow mouth is important for containing the aroma that rises from the whisky, so that when we nose it we get the maximum fragrance.*

However, if the only glass you can get your hands on is a sherry copita or brandy snifter, these will work just as well.

A small investment in a properly shaped glass, such as the *Glencairn Glass*, will increase your enjoyment of single malt Scotch whisky immensely.

One last thing – there is a distinct difference between *tasting* and *drinking*. The following steps detail a procedure for tasting a single malt Scotch whisky so that you can compare it to others.

Covered tasting glass

Drinking whisky is the act of enjoying the dram of your choice – which may be done at any time, any place and (gasp) with ice and/or the mixer of your choice. In my estimation, you will be destroying a perfectly good single malt, but, you bought it – it is yours, so drink it however you like.

The tasting process

While there is a lot of unnecessary pomp and circumstance associated with a traditional Scotch whisky tasting, at the core there is good reason to follow a prescribed and repeatable method. Following the same steps each time you try a whisky allows you to more easily and objectively compare it to any Scotch whisky you subsequently try.

Whether you are taking part in a tasting with a group or in the privacy of your home, you may want to take notes on the whisky after each step - but this is by no means a requirement.

The tasting process is broken down into three basic parts: Appearance, Nose, and Taste & Finish.

1. Appearance

Pour in a measure of whisky - about an ounce.

Tilt your glass, hold it up to the light, and examine the color. Some of the common colors that have been used to describe whiskies are: white wine, yellow, very pale, pale, pale gold, gold, old gold, full gold, bronze, pale amber, amber, and full amber.

Remember, though, that the color of a whisky can not be relied upon to tell you about its flavor. While an older whisky might very well have a darker color, a lighter color doesn't automatically indicate a lighter style or a younger whisky.

When first distilled, whisky is a clear liquid - it obtains all of its color* from the cask in which it is aged. Malts aged

---

* *Except when artificially colored through the addition of spirit caramel.*

---

in bourbon casks usually have a lighter, more golden color, while those aged in sherry casks are generally a bit darker and amber colored.

There are other factors that may influence the color. As previously mentioned, distillers are allowed to add small amounts of coloring (in the form of caramel) in order to ensure that each batch has a consistent color.

Also, many whiskies are subjected to the *chill-filtration process* - a process wherein after aging, but prior to bottling, the whisky is chilled. The drop in temperature causes proteins to coalesce, which results in some cloudiness in the whisky. The whisky is then filtered to remove the cloudiness and bottled. Chill-filtration can alter the color as well as the flavor of the whisky. Unless the label on your bottle states that the contents have *not* been chill filtered, you can safely assume that it *has been* chill filtered.

Back to the tasting. Tilt your glass to wet the sides. Notice that like wine, whisky has "legs." The faster the legs roll down, the lighter the body of the whisky; the slower, the more full-bodied the whisky.

2. Nose
Strange as it may sound, a whisky is tasted primarily with the nose. The aroma indicates the character and strength of the whisky, and even an untrained nose should be able to identify some very specific scents in a glass of whisky.

Aroma (undiluted)
Swirl the whisky in the glass and take a sniff. If it has been bottled directly from the cask it may be as much as 63% alcohol, and taking too powerful a sniff can numb your

---

sense of smell for a short time. You can actually burn your olfactory nerves by sniffing too strongly! So, be careful with your initial smell.

At this point (even though we are still in the nosing phase) you may want to take a small, quick sip. This is to give you a baseline flavor for that particular whisky.

Aroma (diluted)
Now add a little water.

Why? Two reasons. First, the addition of even a few drops of water can change the whisky, releasing new aromas and flavors. Second, the water is used to dilute very strong whisky and reduce the alcohol "bite" that could easily overwhelm a developing palate.

It is preferable to use bottled spring water, though tap water will do in a pinch. NEVER use carbonated water.

Some people will tell you that the mix should be 50% whisky - 50% water - this level of dilution is generally used by professional tasters. I always start with a very small amount of water (a few drops) and add from there. I have rarely added so much water to the point where a whisky has been diluted by half.

The key is to simply find what works for you AND what works for each particular whisky. Experiment: add a little water - nose - taste - add a little more - until you feel the whisky tastes and smells its best.

Different whiskies will take different levels of dilution – older whiskies (15 years old or more) tend to require less water, as do lighter whiskies. As a general rule, younger (10 year old), and very peaty whiskies (Laphroaig, Ardbeg, and

Lagavulin, for example) can stand up to more water. Any whisky can be damaged by too much water - the aromas tend to fall apart and the flavor becomes flat.

You may find it difficult to describe the aromas, but if you are participating in a group tasting, don't be afraid to share your thoughts. You'll find that when you come up with an accurate description, other tasters will agree, or make their own observations with which you may agree.

Here's a little trick that may help as you learn to discern new flavors. This is particularly useful for novices who can't detect anything in the nose other than "whisky".

1. Hold the tasting glass in one hand, while completely covering the mouth of the glass with your other hand.
2. Vigorously swirl/shake the glass - this will aerate the heck out of the whisky. The palm of your hand should get wet.
3. Put down the glass and rub the palms of your hands together - this should be done quickly to generate a little heat and cause the whisky to evaporate.
4. Immediately cup your hands and place them over your nose and mouth. Take a deep sniff.

You should now be able to detect at least one of the more distinct "non-whisky" aspects of the nose.

3. Taste & Finish

Mouth-Feel

Take a large sip, and then roll it over your tongue. First, note the *texture* of the whisky. It may be smooth, light, oily, thick, astringent, dry, or any of a hundred other descriptors.

You then want to identify the primary tastes - there are only four: sweet, salty, sour, and bitter. Most whiskies will present a mixture - sometimes balanced, sometimes not.

Carefully breathe out through your nose now (you should still have the whisky in your mouth at this point).

Overall taste

What other flavors can you detect? This is where it can get interesting - chocolate, apple, banana, honey, heather, wood, and even grass have been used to describe the flavors people detect in whisky.

Are the flavors consistent with your original perception based on the whisky's aroma, or has some new flavor come through? Tasting whisky is about exploring the interdependence of aroma and taste.

Finish

Swallow and take a moment to think about the flavor. Does the flavor linger, or does it fade rapidly? Does a new taste appear, or does an existing taste change or reassert itself? Is there any after taste, pleasant or unpleasant?

If taking notes, jot your thoughts down. If you have more whisky left in your glass, you may wish to repeat the tasting process. You may notice that the flavor changes - for better or worse, and sometimes quite dramatically - especially if your glass remains uncovered between sips.

Drink something to clear your palate, a spring water or carbonated water, and move along to the next sample.

Don't panic...

If you are tasting several whiskies, don't be disappointed if you cannot discern between them.

At many of the tastings I host, I have a number of first-timers who swear they can not differentiate between most of the single malts. It's not until I pull out one of the smoky Islay whiskies that these novices can detect a noticeable difference.

To a new taster, there is very little difference between the various Speyside and Highland whiskies. This is to be expected and is perfectly understandable.

When you are first getting started, you may want to limit your tasting to no more than one or two whiskies at a time.

Be patient. Your palate will develop with time and experience.

After the tasting

Once you are done with the formal part of the tasting, it's time to enjoy the whiskies in a more relaxed way. Choose the whisky you enjoyed the most and pour yourself a few ounces.

Chocolate, cheese, and smoked salmon are three things which go well with single malt Scotch whisky. As for me, I recommend a good chocolate chip cookie as an accompaniment to just about any whisky. The whisky enhances the flavors in the cookie, and the cookie adds a great dimension to the whisky.

If you remember nothing else...

There are three basic components of tasting: Appearance, Nose, Taste & Finish.

The best glass to taste whisky in is a tulip-shaped glass, though a brandy glass will work well.

Water should be added to dilute the whisky. How much you add is a matter of personal preference, but older whiskies tend to require less water, as do lighter whiskies. Younger (10 year old), and very peaty whiskies can take a lot more water.

When diluting, use bottled water; never carbonated.

When tasting, ice or soda water should never be added to single malt Scotch - not only will it mask the taste, it can destroy it.

Accompany your whisky with chocolate chip cookies - you won't regret it.

Too much of anything
is bad, but too much of
good whisky is barely
enough.

Mark Twain

Chapter 6

What Will I Like?

What will you like? That is an excellent question, and one that I cannot answer.

I could certainly tell you what I like, but your tastes could be, and probably are, quite different than mine.

If you are looking for someone to tell you what *they* like, you will not have to go very far - most of the books currently available on the topic dedicate a number of pages to exhaustive listings of distilleries and the tasting notes of the authors. ***That is decidedly not the purpose of this book.***

First, any listing of all of the distilleries that are producing, bottling, and distributing, would, in the end, be of very little use to a novice Scotch whisky drinker.

Secondly, although I certainly have opinions, I tend to stay away from making judgements on the various whiskies produced, as this is a completely subjective endeavor. I encourage you to make your own judgements. Everyone's tastes are different, and what I believe to be a fantastic whisky might taste like pond water to you.

I often have people sheepishly tell me that their Scotch whisky of choice is Dewar's (a blend), or one of the lighter single malts - as if they expect me to disapprove and try to convert them to some heavier whisky.

I simply say "Drink what you like."

To prove a point, in the next chapter I'll provide you with tasting notes from several very prominent sources who rate the same bottle of whisky. You will see how, even among experts, opinions vary.

The beauty of single malt is that there is very likely at least one that will suit your tastes.

Don't worry though, I won't leave you high and dry. There are at least two ways (in addition to trying as many whiskies as possible) to figure out what you might like.

What sells best

Best selling might easily be attributed to best distribution or best marketing, but it does not necessarily mean best tasting. However, when you come right down to it, there *is* a reason these whiskies are on the best selling list - a lot of people drink a lot of it.

Top Selling Brands of single malt Scotch (USA)
2004 data

The Glenlivet
Glenfiddich
The Macallan
The Balvenie

Starting out with the best sellers is a reliable way to introduce yourself to whiskies which are readily available, very consistent, well-regarded, and well-liked.

What they taste like

As I stated, this book is not about providing information on the all of the distillers and their products. I will *instead* provide you with a very brief listing of some of the distilleries you are likely to encounter as you start to enjoy single malt Scotch whisky. This includes what's probably available in your local liquor store or your favorite high-end restaurant.

The following distilleries are reliable, produce Scotch whisky that you'll readily find, and among them, offer a range of flavors well worth trying.

Speyside

Aberlour
Balvenie
Cragganmore
Glenfarclas
Glenfiddich
Glenrothes
The Glenlivet
Macallan

Highland

Dalmore
Dalwhinnie
Glenmorangie
Highland Park
Isle of Jura
Oban
Scapa
Talisker

Islay

Ardbeg
Bowmore
Bruichladdich
Bunnahabhain
Lagavulin
Laphroaig

Lowland

Auchentoshan
Glenkinchie

Once you have tried the offerings from one or two of these distillers, your next question will invariably be: *"If I like a particular malt whisky, what other whiskies might I also enjoy?"* And lucky you, a PhD in Classification Methodology (honest!) decided to answer this question.

Dr. Wishart does the unspeakable, and ignores classifying single malts by region, instead focusing on classification by flavor. The result was ten clusters of single malt whiskies grouped by identifying similar flavors among 12 flavor traits.

Cluster A
Full-Bodied, Medium-Sweet, Pronounced Sherry with Fruity, Spicy, Malty Notes and Nutty, Smoky Hints.
Dalmore, Macallan, Balmenach, Dailuaine, Glendronach, Mortlach, Royal Lochnagar

Cluster B
Medium-Bodied, Medium-Sweet, with Nutty, Malty, Floral, Honey and Fruity Notes
Aberlour, Cragganmore, Glenfarclas, Scapa, Aberfeldy, Ben Nevis, Benrinnes, Benromach, Blair Athol, Edradour, Glencadam, Glenturret, Knockando, Longmorn, Strathisla

Cluster C
Medium-Bodied, Medium-Sweet, with Fruity, Floral, Honey, Malty Notes and Spicy Hints
Balvenie, Dalwhinnie, The Glenlivet, Benriach, Clynelish, Glendullan, Glen Elgin, Glen Ord, Linkwood, Royal Brackla

Cluster D

Light, Medium-Sweet, Low or No Peat, with Fruity, Floral, Malty Notes and Nutty Hints

Auchentoshan, An Cnoc, Isle of Arran, Aultmore, Cardhu, Glengoyne, Glen Grant, Glentauchers, Mannochmore, Speyside, Tamdhu, Tobermory

Cluster E

Light, Medium-Sweet, Low Peat, with Floral, Malty Notes and Fruity, Spicy, Honey Hints

Bunnahabhain, Glenkinchie, Allt a Bhainne, Bladnoch, Braeval, Caperdonich, Glenallachie, Glenburgie

Cluster F

Medium-Bodied, Medium-Sweet, Low Peat, Malty Notes and Sherry, Honey, Spicy Hints

Glenrothes, Ardmore, Auchroisk, Deanston, Glen Deveron, Glen Keith, Fettercairn, Tomatin, Tormore, Tullibardine

Cluster G

Medium-Bodied, Sweet, Low Peat and Floral Notes

Glenfiddich, Dufftown, Glen Spey, Miltonduff, Speyburn

Cluster H

Medium-Bodied, Medium-Sweet, with Smoky, Fruity, Spicy Notes and Floral, Nutty Hints

Glenmorangie, Oban, Balblair, Craigellachie, Glen Garioch, Old Pulteney, Strathmill, Tamnavulin, Teaninich

Cluster I
Medium-Light, Dry, with Smoky, Spicy, Honey Notes and Nutty, Floral Hints
Bowmore, Bruichladdich, Highland Park, Isle of Jura, Glen Scotia, Springbank

Cluster J
Full-Bodied, Dry, Pungent, Peaty and Medicinal, with Spicy, Feinty Notes
Ardbeg, Lagavulin, Laphroaig, Talisker, Caol Ila

If you develop an interest in single malt, I highly recommend that this is the next book you purchase:

Whisky Classified: Choosing Single Malts by Flavour by David Wishart, published by Pavilion Books, London 2006.

Strathisla - The oldest operating distillery in the Highlands

What Will I Like?

Chapter 7
Whose Tasting Notes?

As you continue to explore Scotch whisky, you'll discover books which feature the tasting notes of the author. Different authors may have vastly different styles, as well as different opinions on whiskies.

To see how experts can disagree on a whisky, I've included tasting notes from books by several well-known, well-respected experts and their opinions of **Dalwhinnie 15-year-old**.

Michael Jackson
Complete Guide to Single Malt Scotch, 5th Edition
Running Press Book Publishers, 2004

Color: Bright gold

Nose: Very aromatic, dry, faintly phenolic, lightly peaty

Body: Firm, slightly oily

Palate: Remarkably smooth, long lasting flavor development. Aromatic, heather-honey notes give way to cut-grass, malty sweetness which intensifies to a sudden burst of peat.

Finish: A long crescendo

Rating: 76 out of 100

Jim Murray
Jim Murray's Whiskey Bible 2005
Carlton Books, 2004

Nose: Sublime stuff: a curious mixture of coke smoke and peat-reek wafts teasingly over the gently honied malt. A hint of melon offers some fruit but the caressing malt stars.

Taste: That rarest of combinations: at once silky and malt intense, yet at the same time peppery and tin-hat time for the taste buds, but the silk wins out and a sheen of barley sugar coats everything, soft peat included.

Finish: Some cocoa and coffee notes, yet the pervading honied sweetness means that there is no bitterness that cannot be controlled.

Balance: One of the most complete mainland malts of them all. Know anyone who reckons they don't like whisky? Give them a glass of this. Oh, if only the average masterpiece could be this good.

Rating: 94 out of 100

Ian Wisniewski
Classic Malt Whisky
Prion, 2001

Nose: Fruity, citrus zest with vanilla, caramel, oakey spice and smokey hints

Taste: Subtle peaty, smokey notes on the palate, with creamy, heather honey, fudge notes and citrus freshness

Finish: Soft heathery finish

David Wishart
Whisky Classified
Pavilion, 2006

Nose: Sweet, nutty aroma with a floral edge hinting of smoke and marmalade.

Taste: Fresh and heathery, citrus fruits, honey, vanilla and a whiff of peat.

Official Tasting Notes
Dalwhinnie

Nose: A smooth yet dry nose with hints of heather and peat.

Taste: Mellow, soft and lasting flavours of heather, honey sweetness and vanillas followed by deeper citrus-fruit flavours and hints of malted bread.

Finish: Long, lingering yet gentle finish that starts with sweetness but gives way to smoke, peat and malt.

These are five different views of the same whisky. Which one is right? They all are, because despite coming from experts, they are still subjective opinions. You may have a view of Dalwhinnie which is different than any of these.

Whose tasting notes should you use? Your own! That's the beauty of enjoying whisky; you decide what you like.

At the back of this book, I've provided several pages for you to begin taking your own tasting notes.

Chapter 8
A Word About Blends

While this book is about tasting and enjoying single malt whiskies, it's important to take a moment to talk about the blended whiskies. This gives a sense of history - it also shows that although single malts predate blends, it was the interest in blended whisky which kept the production of single malt going.

You should also understand that while there tends to be a bias among single malt snobs against blends, there are a number of blends which are quite good.

Much of what you have read in this book is also applicable towards gaining an appreciation for blends. Personally, it was only after understanding single malt, did I fully begin to understand the nuances that blends can offer.

What is blended whisky?

In 1831 Aeneas Coffey improved upon a device known as a *patent* or *continuous* still, which enabled a continuous process of distillation to take place. This is in contrast to pot stills which are used to distill spirit in batches.

This led to the wide scale production of grain whisky - a different, less intense drink than the malt whisky produced in those distinctive copper pot stills. Corn, wheat and unmalted barley are the primary grains, though it doesn't seem to matter much which.

The lighter flavored grain whisky, when blended with the stronger, more robust single malts, extended the appeal of Scotch whisky to a considerably wider market. This blended product is referred to as, simply enough, *blended Scotch whisky*.

What many people don't realize is that most of the single malt whisky distilled today (as much as 90% of all single malts) is *not* bottled or sold as single malt Scotch whisky, but instead is used in the production of blended whisky.

What's in a blend?

The whisky industry is a convoluted and incestuous one. Large conglomerates, like *Pernod-Ricard* and *Diageo*, now own a majority of the once independent distilleries. They also own a number of the blended brands. As a result, most blends include single malt product produced at a distillery which is also owned by the parent company.

A blended Scotch whisky can be made up of as many as 50 individual single malt and grain whiskies and theoretically as few as two. Johnnie Walker Red apparently contains 35 different single malts. For some reason, blenders do not always like to disclose exactly which single malts are included in their product.

There is no evidence of a legal dictate that specifies the minimum amount of single malt that must be used in a blended whisky.

The law *does* dictate that, like single malt Scotch whisky, the declared age on the label of a blended whisky must refer to the youngest whisky in the bottle. If a blend is described as being 12 years old, the youngest whisky in that blend must have been matured for at least 12 years (this includes the grain whisky components). If there is no age declared on the bottle, then the youngest whisky will have been aged at least 3 years. It is very likely that even the single malts in the blend will have been aged far less than ten years.

Top Selling Brands of Blended Scotch (USA)
Dewar's (Bacardi)
Johnnie Walker (Diageo)
J&B (Diageo)
Chivas Regal (Pernod-Ricard)
Cutty Sark (Berry Bros & Rudd)

Drinking blends

Blended whisky can have a substantially different taste than single malt whisky and, unlike single malt, is usually taken over ice or mixed with soda water, cola beverages, fruit juices or another mixer.

There are a number of classic cocktails which have been created to showcase the flavors of blended Scotch whisky. I've included several in the next chapter.

There's no such thing
as bad whisky.
Some whiskies just
happen to be better
than others.

William Faulkner, Author

Chapter 9

Whisky Cocktails

In this chapter, we'll fly in the face of tradition and celebrate the art of the cocktail. Classic whisky cocktails often call for a blended Scotch, bourbon, Irish, or Canadian whisk(e)y. Feel free to use any whisky at hand.

Classic cocktails

Black Watch

Ingredients:
1 1/2 ounces Scotch whisky
1/2 ounce coffee liqueur (Kahlua)

Mixing instructions:
Pour the Scotch whisky and coffee liqueur into an old-fashioned glass almost filled with ice cubes. Stir.

Gale Warning

Ingredients:
2 ounces Scotch whisky
Cranberry juice
Pineapple juice

Mixing instructions:
Fill glass with ice, add Scotch whisky. Fill glass with equal parts Cranberry and Pineapple juice. Stir.

Godfather

Ingredients:
1 1/2 ounces Scotch whisky
1/2 Amaretto

Mixing instructions:
Fill glass with ice, add Scotch whisky and amaretto. Stir.

London Sour

Ingredients:
2 ounces Scotch whisky
Dash of orange Curaçao (or Triple Sec)
Dash of orange juice
Sour mix

Mixing instructions:
Fill rocks glass with ice, add Scotch whisky, orange Curaçao, orange juice. Fill with Sour mix. Shake.

Old Fashioned

Ingredients:
2 ounces Scotch whisky
1 teaspoon sugar
1-3 dashes Angostura bitters
1 slice lemon
1 slice orange

Mixing instructions:

Muddle the sugar, lemon, orange, and bitters in an old-fashioned glass. Stir well. Add Scotch whisky and stir. Add a twist of lemon peel and ice cubes. Top with a cherry. (Some recipes call for the addition of water or club soda).

Rob Roy/Manhattan

Ingredients:
1 1/2 ounces Scotch whisky

3/4 ounce sweet vermouth
1-3 dashes Angostura bitters

Mixing instructions:
Stir the Scotch whisky, vermouth, and bitters (with ice); strain into a cocktail glass. Garnish with a cherry.

Rusty Nail

Ingredients:
1 1/2 ounces Scotch whisky
1/2 ounce Drambuie

Mixing instructions:
Pour the Scotch whisky and Drambuie into an old-fashioned glass almost filled with ice cubes. Stir well. Garnish with a lemon peel.

Scottish Coffee

Ingredients:
1 ounce Scotch whisky
1 ounce Drambuie
Black Coffee

Mixing instructions:
Pour the Scotch whisky and Drambuie into an mug. Fill with black coffee. Top with whipped cream and garnish with shaved chocolate.

Whisky Sour

Ingredients:
2 ounces Scotch whisky
Juice of 1/2 lemon
1/2 teaspoon powdered sugar

Mixing instructions:
Shake Scotch whisky, lemon juice, and powdered sugar (with ice) and strain into a glass. Garnish with half-slice of lemon, top with a cherry.

Signature cocktails

In addition to the classic whisky cocktails, more and more bartenders are rising to the challenge to create new cocktails that complement the strong flavors of Scotch whisky - instead of trying to cover it up. Here are some signature recipes from bartenders around the world.

Highland Cooler
Ethan Kelley, The Brandy Library, New York City, USA

Ingredients:
1 ounce Famous Grouse
2 ounces Ginger beer
1 1/2 ounces Drambuie
1/2 ounce lime juice, unsweetened
1 dash Angostura bitters

Mixing instructions:
Place all ingredients in a shaker; shake vigorously, strain into a highball over fresh ice. Garnish with lime slice.

Speyside Sazerac
Rob Poulter, Raoul's Bar, Oxford, UK

Ingredients:
2 ounces Glenfiddich Solera Reserve
1/2 ounce Cointreau
1/2 ounce Vanilla syrup
1 dash Peychaurds bitters

Mixing instructions:
Fill a rocks glass with crushed ice, add Cointreau. Let chill. In a tall glass filled with ice, add other ingredients, and stir. Discard ice and Cointreau from rocks glass - Strain the contents of the tall glass into the rocks glass.

Burnt Island

Darcy O'Neil, The Art of Drink, Ontario, Canada

Ingredients:
1 1/4 ounces Glenlivet 12
1/2 ounce Vanilla Bols
1/4 ounce Cinnamon Vodka
3/4 ounce Dark Caramel Syrup
1 1/4 ounces Club Soda
1 dash Angostura bitters

Mixing instructions:
Place all ingredients, except club soda, in a shaker; shake and strain into a glass filled with ice. Top-off with club soda.

Perfect Manhattan

Julien Gualdoni, Trailer Happiness, London, UK

Ingredients:
1 1/2 ounces Glenrothes Special Reserve
1/2 ounce Noilly Dry vermouth
3/4 ounce Noilly Red vermouth
Dash Angostura Bitter
1/3 ounce Maraschino cherry juice

Mixing instructions:
Put ice into a mixing glass and rinse the ice with Angostura Bitter. Add all ingredients and stir; strain into a martini glass. Garnish with a lemon twist

The Drunken Sailor

Mike Miller, Delilah's, Chicago, USA

Ingredients:
1 ounce Laphroaig 10 (preferably Cask Strength)
1 ounce Blanco Mezcal
Dash Midori

Splash of Sour Mix
Squeeze of Fresh Lime

Mixing instructions:
Combine the ingredients in a shaker with ice, shake fairly hard
and serve in a martini glass. Garnish with a cherry.

The Secret Monkey

Mickael Perron, BarNowOn, London, UK

Ingredients:
1 1/2 ounces Monkey Shoulder
3/4 ounce Watermelon liqueur
1 ounce Apple juice
1 Lime wedge squeeze

Mixing instructions:
Place all ingredients into a cocktail shaker. Shake; serve straight
up in a martini glass. Grate cinnamon on top as garnish.

The Debonair

Gary Regan, renowned cocktail expert & author
From "The Joy of Mixology" (reprinted with permission)

Ingredients:
2 1/2 ounces Oban or Springbank single malt Scotch
1 ounce Original Canton Delicate Ginger Liqueur

Mixing instructions:
Stir and strain into a chilled cocktail glass. Garnish with lemon
twist.

*My wife and I came up with this one in the early nineties. It's based on
the Whisky Mac, a somewhat popular drink in the UK that calls for scotch
and green ginger wine. If you can't get ginger liqueur in your neck of the
woods, experiment with green ginger wine instead. I suggest two bottlings
of single malt here, chosen for their briny characteristics that play well off
the ginger liqueur, and remember that if you use any bottling other than
the ones suggested here, you'll have to play around with ratios to get the
right balance.*

Chapter 10
Questions, Facts & Terms

Questions

Where does the word "whisky" come from?

It's a corruption of Uisge Beatha (Scots Gaelic) or Usque Baugh (Irish Gaelic) for "water of life" and is pronounced 'Ooshki Baah'.

How much malt is there in a blended whisky?

Most blended whisky contain anywhere from 15% to 60% malt whisky. It varies from one blend to another.

Is a blended whisky with a higher content of malt better than a blend with a low content?

If we compare products at the same age, the one with the higher content of malt is likely to be smoother. The flavor also depends on the quality of the single malt component. "Better" is subjective.

Why do whisky distillers use casks that have previously contained other products?

Historically, the Scots used whatever cask was at hand because it was economical to do so. This was generally, but not always, a cask which had previously stored another spirit. Originally maturation was not a factor, as the cask was simply a transport device. But eventually it was discovered that 1. aging the whisky gave it color and flavor, 2. using new casks overpowered the maturing whisky, and 3. casks which had previously stored another spirit imparted new desirable colors, aromas and flavors to the whisky.

What is peat and its function in the production of malt whisky?

Peat is the result of thousands of years of decomposition of natural elements such as grass and vegetables in the soil and has long been used in Scotland as a source of fuel. It is used to smoke the malting barley. You should know that peat is NOT necessary in the production of whisky. Peat is not used to smoke the barley in the production of Irish whiskey, even though Ireland has just as much peat as Scotland. Instead, Irish distillers use closed kilns to dry the barley using hot, dry air.

Does the whisky continue to mature once it is in the bottle?

Unlike wine, once it's taken from the cask and bottled, whisky does not continue to mature. A 10 year old whisky bottled 15 years ago is **not** a 25 year old whisky.

Is an older whisky better than a younger one?

The 'older is better' attitude that some people take towards whisky doesn't necessarily hold true. Older whiskies can be fantastic, but after resting in a barrel for 20 years or more, the spirit can be overpowered by the wood.

What is the minimum age for Scotch whisky?

The age of the whisky refers to how long it has spent maturing in its oak barrel. In Scotland, whisky must mature for a minimum of 3 years before it's even allowed to be called whisky. Few serious whisky-lovers, though, would touch something so young.

What does an age statement mean?

The age shown on the bottle is the age of the youngest whisky in the bottle. If it's vatted or a blend, there may be older whiskies in the blend.

Can maturation take place outside Scotland?

No. Maturation must take place in Scotland. It is against international law to call it Scotch whisky if it has not been aged in Scotland.

How many distilleries are there?

There are around 90 distilleries in Scotland; but the number which are in production can vary from year to year.

What is the top selling whisky?

Johnnie Walker Red is the best selling Scotch whisky in the world. Glenfiddich is the best selling single malt Scotch whisky in the world. Glenmorangie is the best selling single malt in Scotland. The Glenlivet is the best selling single malt in the U.S.

Facts

- Seven flavor compounds have been identified in cheese, while over 80 have been identified in single malt.

- There are almost half as many distilleries today than there where in 1881 - producing seven times the volume.

- Total single malt Scotch production in 2005 was 700 million liters. 549 million liters of that was used in blends, while 151 million liters was bottled as single malt.

- Production destined for single malt has doubled in 40 years.

- 10% of all Scotch whisky sold is single malt.

- Grain whisky is 40% cheaper to make than single malt whisky.

- 50% of all distilleries are located in Speyside.

- Producing one liter of new spirit requires approximately 13 litres of water and 2.5 kg of barley.

- Producing one bottle of 10 year old whisky requires approximately 4.5 litres water & .8 kg barley.

- There are approximately 18,500,000 barrels of whisky maturing in Scotland.

- Worldwide, Glenfiddich sells 800,000 cases a year. The Glenlivet (second in worldwide sales) currently sells 360,000.

Terms

Alcohol by volume (ABV)

Alcohol by volume (ABV) is an indication of the percentage of alcohol in a beverage.

Coffey (Column or Continuous or Patent) Still

The continuous still, which came into use in the early 19th century, consists of a tall cylindrical column filled with perforated plates. During distillation, water-rich vapors condense onto the plates, while alcohol-enriched vapors pass through.

Dram

A generic term for a poured measure of whisky. For most intents and purposes, a dram may be considered to be one to two ounces.

Grist

A dry mixture of barley malts which have been ground into a coarse flour-like consistency.

Low Wines

The name given to the result of the first distillation. Low wines have an alcoholic content of about 25%.

Malt

Barley which has been soaked in water, allowed to begin to germinate, and then dried. This promotes the conversion of starches to fermentable sugars.

Mash Bill

The components and percentages of grains used when making a mash.

Mash Tun

The tank where grist is mixed with water and heated in order to extract the sugar and other solubles.

New Make Spirit

The final result of distillation, this colorless liquid generally has an ABV of 70%.

Wash

A beer-like liquid created by mixing wort and yeast and allowing to ferment.

Wort

A sugary liquid created by mixing malted barley grist with hot water.

Whisky/Whiskey

An alcoholic beverage distilled from grain, which has then been aged in wooden barrels.

Chapter 11

How To Say It

Aberlour .... *aber-LAU-er*

Ardbeg .... *ard-BEG*

Auchentoshan........................... *OK-en-TOE-shen*

Auchroisk .... *oth-RUSK*

Balvenie .... *bal-VEH-nee*

Bruichladdich .... *brewch-LADDIE*

Bunnahabhain........................... *BOON-a-hah-vun*

Caol Ila .... *cull EE-la*

Cardhu... *kar-DOO*

Clynelish .... *KLINE-leash*

Cragganmore .... *crag-an-MORE*

Craigellachie.............................. *cra-GAL-ach-ee*

Dailuaine...................................... *dall-YEW-in*

Edradour....................................... *edra-DOWER*

Glenfarclas .... *glen-FAR-cles*

Glenfiddich .... *glen-FID-ick*

Glen Garioch............................. *GLEN GEE-ree*

Glenkinchie	.............................glen-KIN-chee
Glenmorangie .	glen-MOR-angee (rhymes with "orangey")
Glenrothes	...................................glen-ROTH-is
Islay	....EYE-luh
Kilchoman	.... kil-HO-man
Knockando	.... knock-AN-dew
Jura	.... Jer-ra
Lagavulin	.... lagga-VOO-lin
Laphroaig	.... la-FROYg
Macallan	.... ma-CAL-an
Oban	.... O-bun
Old Pulteney	.... OLD Pult-nay
Slainte (Gaelic for 'Health!')	.............SCHLAN-ja
Slainte Mhor (Great Health!)	..... SCHLAN-ja VOR
Strathisla	.... strath-EYE-luh
Talisker	.... TAL-is-ker
Tamnavulin	.... TAM-na-VOO-lin
Teaninich	.... TEA-a-NIN-ick
Tullibardine	.... tul-lee-BAR-deen
Uisge Beatha/ Usque Baugh	...............OOSH-ki baah

Suggested Reading

Dave Broom
Handbook of Whisky
Hamlyn, 2000

Michael Jackson
Complete Guide to Single Malt Scotch, 5th Edition
Running Press Book Publishers, 2004

Whisky: The Definitive World Guide
Dorling Kindersley, 2005

Charles MacLean
MacLean's Miscellany Of Whisky
Little Books, 2004

Scotch Whisky: A Liquid History
Cassell, 2004

Jim Murray
Jim Murray's Whiskey Bible 2006
Carlton Books, 2005

Gary Regan
The Joy of Mixology
Clarkson Potter, 2003

David Wishart
Whisky Classified: Choosing Single Malts by Flavour
Pavilion Books, London 2006

Ian Wisniewski
Classic Malt Whisky
Prion, 2001

Name..Age ....

Region/Location .... ABV ....

⚯ Appearance ....

....

....

⚯ Nose..

Undiluted...

....

Diluted ....

....

⚯ Taste

Mouth-feel ....

....

Taste..

....

⚯ Finish ....

....

⚯ Notes ....

....

....

Name..Age ....

Region/Location ....ABV ....

֍ Appearance ....

....

....

֍ Nose...

Undiluted...

....

Diluted ....

....

֍ Taste

Mouth-feel ....

....

Taste...

....

֍ Finish ....

....

֍ Notes ....

....

....

Name.. Age ....

Region/Location .... ABV ....

꙳ Appearance ....

....

....

꙳ Nose...

Undiluted..

....

Diluted ....

....

꙳ Taste

Mouth-feel ....

....

Taste..

....

꙳ Finish ....

....

꙳ Notes ....

....

....

Name..Age ....

Region/Location .... ABV ....

꒱ Appearance ....

....

....

꒱ Nose..

Undiluted...

....

Diluted ....

....

꒱ Taste

Mouth-feel ....

....

Taste...

....

꒱ Finish ....

....

꒱ Notes ....

....

....

Name.. Age ....

Region/Location .... ABV ....

 ⚘ **Appearance** ....

....

....

 ⚘ **Nose**...

Undiluted..

....

Diluted ....

....

 ⚘ **Taste**

Mouth-feel ....

....

Taste...

....

 ⚘ **Finish** ....

....

 ⚘ **Notes** ....

....

....

Your notes...

Your notes...

Also Available from Doceon Press

The Instant Expert's Scotch Tasting Notebook

The Instant Expert's Scotch Tasting Notebook
is a pocket-sized personal tasting journal for
Scotch lovers to record their tasting notes.

Kevin Erskine is a native of New York City,
who now resides in Richmond, Virginia.
He writes the popular Scotch whisky industry news
and commentary web site The Scotch Blog.

The Scotch Blog
www.thescotchblog.com

Straight News. Blunt Comment. No B.S.